BENGAL CATS

D1284310

The Comprehensive Guide on Bengal Cats Choosing, Care, Training, Housing and More

Dr. LEAH AMBROSE

Table of Contents

CHAPTER ONE

INTRODUCTION

Bengal cats are a smart, athletic breed known for their vibrantly striped coats. They are friendly and gentle pets that are descended from domestic cats and wild Asian leopard cats.

HISTORY OF BENGAL CAT

The Bengal cat is a cross between a domestic cat (Felis silvestris catus) and a leopard cat (Felis silvestris catus) (Prionailurus bengalensis). Except for the bigger, snapping eyes, noticeable whisker pads, longer legs, and vivid leopard-style patterns, the leopard cat resembles a domestic cat. It does, in fact, resemble a small leopard.

When a female leopard cat was purchased from a pet store, the Bengal breed was born. Leopard cats could be acquired in pet stores in the United States during the time, unlike today. Due to the specific demands of these cats and state regulations, this is no longer the case. The leopard cat was not purchased with the intention of creating a new breed of cat; rather, Jean Mill wanted a unique pet.

Mill believed her tiny leopard cat looked lonely after a few years, so she got a male domestic cat to provide her company. Her leopard cat had a litter in 1965, absolutely unintentionally and to her amazement. Kin-Kin, a female hybrid kitten, was the only one to survive. Mill sought assistance on how to treat the hybrid from Cornell University College of Veterinary Medicine in Ithaca, New York, and was told that Kin-Kin was most likely infertile. Kin-Kin grew up, married her domestic father, and had two cats, proving that this was not the case. One of the kittens acquired his father's nice domestic nature.

After considerable thought, Mill believed that producing a crossbred breed would help the leopard cats' situation while also providing a suitable and domesticated spotted replacement for the American market. And she set out to accomplish exactly that. It was later discovered that the

Bengal's disposition became more predictable after four generations of separation from the leopard cat. Despite this, there were numerous challenges to conquer along the road. The initial hybrid kittens (also known as F1s) were frequently frightened, cautious cats who grew up to be like their wild cousins. The cats' demeanor became gentle and predictable only when they were several generations removed from the leopard cat. Another reason that hampered the breed's evolution was the fact that, for several generations, the breed could only evolve through the female kittens born, as many hybrids are sterile. Second-generation males (F2s) are also infertile, with only around half of third-generation males (F3s) being viable.

She had enough generations in 1985 to become the Bengal of today. To ensure a gentle, submissive temperament and a happy, healthy domestic cat, current standards require Bengals to be at least four generations old (F4 or more). Except for the CFA, all other associations have fully embraced the Bengal. Bengals have demonstrated to their satisfaction that their attitude is completely domestic and that they pose no threat to anyone in the house. The Bengal has a devoted following today thanks to its exotic appearance and energetic demeanor.

LIFE SPAN OF BENGAL CAT

Bengal cats have a lifespan of 12 to 16 years if they are properly cared for.

Life Expectancy of Bengal Cats is Affected by the Following Factors:

1. Your Bengal cat's diet 2. The amount of activity she receives

3. The quantity and quality of her medical and veterinary care.

4. Pollution and other environmental variables exposure

CHAPTER TWO

PHYSICAL APPEARANCE AND DESCRIPTION OF BENGAL CAT

BODY

Long and robust torso, neither oriental nor foreign. Medium to large in size, although not as big as the largest domestic breed. Boning is tough and unyielding; it's never delicate. One of the most striking qualities is the muscularity, especially in males.

HEAD

With rounded curves and a broad modified wedge. It is wider than it is long. Slightly small in comparison to the rest of the body, but not excessively so. The skull curves gently behind the ears and glides into the neck. The overall appearance of the head differs from that of a domestic cat. In profile, the chin is strong and corresponds with the tip of the nose. With huge, conspicuous whisker pads and high, pronounced cheekbones, the muzzle is full and broad. At the whisker pads, there are minor muzzle fractures. Nose is broad and wide, with a slightly inflated leather nose.

EARS

Medium to small, with a wide base and rounded summits, and a short stature. Set as far to the side as the top of the head, with the frontal view following the shape of the face and the profile view looking ahead. It's not uncommon to find light horizontal furnishings.

EYES

It's almost circular, but it's oval. It's a big place, but it's not infested with bugs. Set wide apart, back into the face, and with a little incline toward the ear's base. Except in the lynx points, eye color is unaffected by coat color. The more color depth and richness, the better.

PAWS & LEGS

Legs are medium length, with the back slightly longer than the front.

Large, round feet with pronounced knuckles.

TAIL

Medium in length, thick at the end, and rounded at the tip.

COAT

Short to medium length. Texture is rich and luxuriant, with a close-lying, unusually smooth and silky feel. Spotted or marbled patterns. Spots are usually random or horizontally oriented. Two unique colors or shades of rosettes. The contrast between the ground color and the pattern is frequently great, resulting in a distinct pattern and sharp edges. Belly is a common sighting.

COLOR

Seal silver tabby, seal silver sepia tabby, seal silver mink tabby, seal silver lynx point, brown tabby, seal sepia tabby, seal mink tabby, seal lynx point, black silver tabby, seal silver sepia tabby, seal silver mink tabby, seal silver lynx point Patterns that are spotted or marbled.

PERSONALITY AND BEHAVIOR

Although the Bengal appears to be a wild cat, others claim that this breed is as lovable and friendly as any domestic cat. Bengals are active, social, energetic cats with a healthy dose of feline curiosity. They are full of life and very people-oriented.

Bengal fans adore the Bengal's charisma and mischievous antics. Bengals create deep links of love and devotion with their family, and they become loyal, affectionate, and fun-loving pals if you meet them halfway and reciprocate their love.

Bengals are athletic and agile, and they enjoy climbing to the highest point in every room. Bengals are frequently excellent sources of amusement. Their intellect is one of the primary features that distinguishes them as friends. It's not surprising that Bengals are as sharp as tacks, given that thriving in the jungle necessitates both intelligence and quick reflexes.

Bengals are quick learners who appreciate learning new skills. In fact, they might pick up on things you don't want them to, like turning on and off light switches, opening doors, and flushing toilets. The inquisitive Bengal is prone to getting into everything, and changes in the home frequently elicit a strong reaction from the Bengal. If you open a cabinet, your Bengal may plunge in for a look, and if the contents aren't up to his standards, he'll rearrange them.

Some Bengals learn to use the toilet due to the leopard cat's habit of eliminating in water to mask their scent from larger predators. Bengals, like their wild relatives, like their freedom and despise being kept or constrained. This is a trait shared by most very active breeds, not only Bengals. Bengals enjoy being near water, especially when it is moving. Some merely run their paws under the faucet once in a while, while others may attempt a frolic in the tub or shower—as long as it's their idea. Some Bengal owners note that their cats' preoccupation with water borders on addiction, and that floods must be avoided at all costs; Bengal owners rapidly learn to keep the toilet lid down.

SIZE OF BENGAL CAT

Bengal cats are often huge cats. Bengal cats can weigh anything from 12 to 22 pounds and stand between 14 and 18 inches tall when fully grown.

CHAPTER THREE

BASIC CARE REQUIREMENT OF BENGAL CAT

NUTRITION

Bengal cats, like their wild siblings, require a meat-based diet, especially if they are from the first three generations. Because most commercial kibble is excessively heavy in carbs, it is not ideal for Bengals.

While these felines can survive on a diet of high-quality canned cat food, the optimal diet for a Bengal cat is either a raw diet or a dried raw diet.

GROOMING

Bengal cats are capable of grooming themselves, but they prefer being groomed and will enjoy brushing on a regular basis.

You should teach your cat to tolerate nail trimming from a

young age, and brush their teeth on a daily basis.

EXERCISE

Bengal cats require significantly more exercise than the normal cat. While most cats spend the majority of their time sleeping, these rambunctious felines require many play sessions every day, especially during their first few years.

When we say Bengal cats have a lot of energy, we really mean it. These cats are known for zipping around the home, jumping on furniture, and not stopping until they've completed numerous laps. Interactive play is vital for your cat's health and will also help you save money on your furniture. Teaser toys, lasers, and battery-operated cat toys are all must-haves for enthusiastic play. Make sure your cat has multiple scratching posts, as well as a towering cat tower that will satisfy their natural desire to climb. The more catification you add to your home, the better.

Bengals are usually content to go on a leash since they have a natural desire to explore. If you want to enjoy this pastime with your Bengal kitten, start teaching them how to walk on a leash at an early age. Safe outdoor exploring is a great way for your cat to get some exercise while also stimulating his or her inquisitive mind.

HEALTH

Bengal cats, like many other cat breeds, can suffer from a variety of health problems. As a Bengal cat grows, it may acquire eye disorders such as cataracts and progressive retinal atrophy (PRA). The genetic form of PRA does not only affect older cats; it can also affect kittens as early as 12 weeks old. There is no known cure for PRA, which causes blindness.

Flat-chested kitten syndrome affects some Bengal kittens. This is usually caught by the breeder, and these cats can live healthy lives with treatment.

Patellar luxation is a joint condition in Bengals that causes the kneecaps to slide to one side. This has an impact on mobility and can be uncomfortable, especially later in life.

Hypertrophic cardiomyopathy is a type of enlarged heart that affects a tiny number of Bengal cats (HCM). While breeders can have their cats tested for cardiac murmurs, it's impossible to anticipate whether future

generations will develop HCM.
There is no such thing as a
breeding line that is free of HCM.

BATHING

Cats, unlike other pets, do not
require bathing on a regular basis.
Bengals also have relatively short
hair, which means they are less
likely to become dirty if they go
outside.

If you do have to bathe your cat,
you won't have too many issues
because the breed is recognized
for its affinity for water. Bathing

your Bengal more than once every 3 to 4 weeks will help to prevent skin problems such as dermatitis.

Bengals brush their body in the same way that other cats do, so they keep themselves clean.

HABITAT/HOUSING

Bengals do not perform well in small areas due of their high activity levels. For people who live in apartments or small studios, they are not the best pets.

Although outside exposure isn't required, your Bengal cat should have access to a balcony or a yard.

In reality, indoor-only cats are far healthier than outdoor cats, so you may protect your Bengal from diseases like parasites and infections from other animals by keeping him indoors.

But that doesn't mean your Bengal will be content being locked up indoors all day, especially if he or she doesn't have enough area to explore.

Keep in mind that these cats enjoy climbing and running around, and they require a lot of vertical space. As a result, you should provide as many cat trees as possible in your home, as well as a cat exercise wheel for Bengals to help them burn off energy. You may also put a cat perch in your window for times when your Bengal wants to look out the window at birds and other wildlife.

If you plan on keeping your Bengal indoors only, we recommend using cat window guards because

Bengals are the type of cats who would jump out of a window if the opportunity arises.

CHAPTER FOUR

THE BENGAL CAT'S DIET

Bengal cats, like other cats, are obligate carnivores with bodies that have evolved to process meat as their principal food source.

They're also superb hunters, and in the wild, they'd eat rats, birds, and lizards to survive. In the wild, leopard cats catch and consume little prey up to twenty times a day, therefore domesticated Bengals may prefer modest but consistent meals. Their carnivorous character should be reflected in the food they eat, therefore it should have enough amounts of:

1.Protein from animals

2.Fat from animals

3.Minerals and vitamins

Your Bengal will acquire all of the nutrients it needs from meat because it is an obligate carnivore, therefore you should avoid commercial foods that employ carb sources to bulk out their goods.

PROTEIN FROM ANIMALS

- Muscle
- Skin
- Coat

To get the nutrition they need to life, cats metabolize the amino acids that proteins are comprised of.

Felines can metabolize vegetable protein, but only inefficiently, so they must consume more to meet their nutritional requirements. Taurine, an amino acid required by cats for eye and heart health, is not found in vegetable protein.

Muscle meat and organs, such as the liver, are the finest sources of animal protein.

FAT FROM ANIMALS

Fat is one of the most important sources of energy for cats, second only to animal protein, and is required for hunting, healing, and breeding. Essential fatty acids, such as

- Linoleic acid
- Omega-3 and omega-6
- Arachidonic acid

These substances aid in the preservation of cell structure and the healing processes of cats.

Cats have evolved to enjoy the flavor of animal fat as hunters, and food containing a significant amount of animal fat will be consumed with relish. Fatty food is especially appealing to pregnant cats.

VITAMINS AND MINERALS

Bengals require the following vitamins in their diet:

TYPE OF VITAMIN: FAT-SOLUTED

VITAMIN A—liver, salmon, egg yolk, and butter are some of the best sources of vitamin A.

VITAMIN D is found in liver, kidneys, fish oil, and eggs.

VITAMIN E—liver, egg, wheat germ oil, milk, and butter are all good sources.

TYPES OF VITAMIN: WATER SOLUBLE

BEST SOURCES OF VITAMINS: VITAMIN B COMPLEX—meat, milk, eggs, and liver

Cats are capable of producing sufficient amounts of vitamins C and K on their own.

A Bengal's diet should also include small amounts of minerals, such as

- zinc.
- Magnesium
- Calcium

All of the nutrients stated above are found in the prey that a wild cat would normally pursue.

CHAPTER FIVE

HEALTH ISSUES AND TREATMENT OF BENGAL CAT

1. EYE DISEASES

Bengal cats have a greater prevalence of eye disorders than many other cat breeds, which many cat owners are astonished to learn. This could be owing to their curious, lively, and active temperament. Their eyesight, for example, may be compromised by myopia, a disorder in which the eyes do not develop enough focusing capacity to see clearly. It may be minor, but a veterinarian may be required to treat it. Because myopia is linked to the retina, it might cause your cat's eyesight to deteriorate. The retina is a membrane that lines the inside of the eyeball and receives light through the lens before sending it to the brain.

Some Bengal cats are genetically predisposed to progressive retinal atrophy, which causes the retina to degenerate and finally blind the cat.

While there is no cure for PRA, laser surgery may be able to save the vision of cats with detached retinas. A retinal detachment can occur as a result of eye trauma or disease. Glaucoma is a disorder in which the pressure inside the eye rises and destroys the optic nerve. This can result in vision loss. Only an eye specialist can address this, so if you have any concerns about your Bengal cat, please contact your veterinarian.

Here Are Some Eye Diseases Associated with Bengal Cats:

- Glaucoma
- Myopia
- Corneal Sequestra
- Cataracts

- Conjunctivitis

- Uveitis

- Retinal Disorders

2. DENTAL PROBLEMS

Tooth problems are one of the most prevalent health issues that Bengal cats confront. Your Bengal cat could have gum disease, which can cause tooth pain, poor dental hygiene, and gum infections. Dental issues in Bengal cats can lead to a thick, yellow-tinted plaque build-up, which can stink up the mouth.

This is one of the very few problems that Bengal cats have, and it is exceedingly rare. They are also less prone than other breeds to have oral ulcers or cancer, which is why it's important to be aware of this risk factor.

3. HIP DYSPLASIA

Hip dysplasia is a hip joint disorder that causes Bengal cats to be lame in their hind legs and makes walking difficult. While these joints are not functioning properly, they may exhibit increased laxity and abnormal movement, which can lead to joint degeneration and severe osteoarthritis over time.

Bengal cats can suffer from patellar luxation, which occurs when the patella (knee cap) slips out of its normal place. This results in a limp or difficulty walking on the back legs. It's possible that surgery will be required to fix the problem.

Hip dysplasia is a condition that affects a variety of cat breeds, not just Bengal cats, and it is known to have a strong heritable component.

4. DIABETES

Diabetes is a condition in which the body's blood sugar (glucose) levels are abnormally high. It's a dangerous disorder that can cause blindness, kidney failure, and even death.

Diabetes in Bengal cats manifests itself in the following ways:

- Extreme thirsty

- Loss of appetite

- High blood glucose levels

- Low urination

- Easily fatigued

- Lethargic Fatigue

- Extreme muscle twitching.

5. KIDNEY DISEASE

Kidney disease is more common in cats than in dogs.

Cats have more renal enzymes in their blood than humans, and the majority of these enzymes are expressed in their urine.

Chronic vomiting, lacerations on the kidneys, and kitty litter feces are all causes of renal disease in Bengal cats. Renal disease can lead to kidney failure in severe circumstances. It can be avoided by having your Bengal cat spayed or vaccinated.

6. RARE DERMATOLOGICAL PROBLEM

Bengal cats, like many other animals, have their own set of skin issues. Bengal cats, on the other hand, are prone to cyclic vomitus, a common dermatological disease. It's essentially uncontrollable vomiting that can happen for no apparent reason.

7. THYROID PROBLEMS

Thyroid problems are one of the most common health problems in Bengal cats.

This can have an immediate effect on their weight, which can lead to a variety of health problems. In the long run, thyroid issues can lead to hyperthyroidism or hypothyroidism.

Weight gain, decreased appetite, vomiting, and sadness are just a few of the symptoms.

The thyroid gland is in charge of creating hormones that keep the human body running smoothly. It aids in the regulation of metabolism.

8. LIVER DISEASE

Liver illness is one of the most common health problems in Bengal cats. Although other cat breeds can get liver problems, Bengal cats are noted for having small livers. One of the key reasons why the breed is more prone to liver disease is because of this.

The reason may be unknown, and there are no obvious symptoms that can be used to relate a cat's liver condition to a specific diet. In Bengal cats, however, there are a few prevalent causes of liver illness.

Among these include feline viral hepatitis, hereditary liver disease, and excessive alcohol and hazardous drug usage.

9. GASTROINTESTINAL DISEASES

Bengal cats are prone to stomach problems. Intestinal and gastrointestinal parasites are the most common causes of these disorders. The difference between the two is the length of time each has an impact on a cat's life. Bengal cats with gastrointestinal parasites have a shorter lifespan than those with intestinal parasites.

10. HYPERTHYROIDISM

Hyperthyroidism is a dangerous disorder in which the thyroid gland secretes enormous amounts of hormones, causing hyperthyroidism symptoms.

If left untreated, this condition can result in hyperactivity, nausea, vomiting, an enlarged heart, and even death.

It is most common in young and elderly female cats between the ages of two and six. The condition is incurable, but it has no impact on the cat's quality of life.

CONCLUSION

You must be committed to the Bengal cat breed and its behavior if you decide to adopt one into your family. Bengals are mischievous, lively, loud, water-loving creatures who desire to be interacted with. If you want a lovely lap cat, don't get a Bengal.

THE END

Made in United States
North Haven, CT
21 February 2023

32948444R00033